THIS JOURNAL BELONGS TO

....

MESSAGE

....

....

....

....

....

GIFT DATE

....

Conscious Transformations
Within Me, Within You

— A HEALING JOURNAL THROUGH POETRY —

By MARLA MAHARAJ

Sharinglightandlove Press
Houston, Texas

Conscious Transformations
Within Me, Within You

First edition: July 2015

Marla Maharaj is sometimes available for poetry readings and speaking engagements. To find out more, email her at **sharinglightandlove@gmail.com**.
Send mail to:
Sharinglightandlove
c/o Marla Maharaj
P.O. Box 711254, Houston, TX 77271
www.sharinglightandlove.com

Softcover ISBN: 978-0-9965022-0-7
Hardcover ISBN: 978-0-9965022-1-4

Cover design and book layout by Barbara Lindenberg, Bluebird Designs, Houston, Texas.

Cover artwork courtesy of Yumna Ali, a senior at DeBakey High School for Health Professions. Author's photograph on back cover by Mindy Tran, a senior at DeBakey High School for Health Professions.

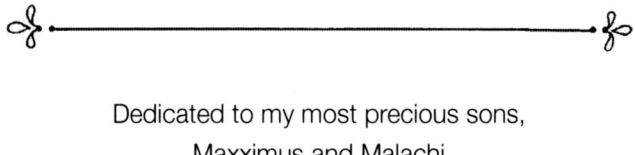

Dedicated to my most precious sons,
Maxximus and Malachi

Acknowledgements

I cannot express my thanks enough to my two sons—Maxximus and Malachi—for being the driving force behind why I chose to not give in when life itself seemed to tear me apart. I chose to be an example of what it looks like when a person anchors themselves in God and never gives up. I wish to teach them to remain unidentified by the storms of life when the raging waves seem to make the ocean feel separate from the water which it's made up of.

Thanks goes to my amazing students at DeBakey High School for Health Professions for giving me the encouragement to move forward in putting these poems together in the form of a journal. With this tool, we can reflect together on some of life's challenges and also share in each other's joys.

My heartfelt thanks to the Self-Realization Fellowship—and the teachings of Paramahansa Yogananda—for introducing and stressing the need for daily meditation and introspection. Thank you for helping me learn to dissect who I am to the very core and for allowing me to make myself empty in such a way that God could now begin to fill me up again. I can now live in the consciousness of God's presence, and I can recognize His Holy Spirit as present in the soul of others and in nature.

To Lakewood Church, Pastor Joel Osteen and family: For over the past twelve years, your inspirational messages and midweek soul-energizing sermons have encouraged me to be the best that I can be. Being a part of this environment and in the atmosphere of such unconditional love truly has set a solid foundation, which has anchored my soul to an unshakeable faith.

Many blessings to the individuals at The Institute for Spirituality and Health in Houston for taking the time to listen to and to read these poems. Thank you for sensing the need for this small mission to be heard of and for allowing me to reach out to others in the way of healing through poetic art. Thank you for broadening the scope of my mind to the true meaning of servant leadership, which has encouraged me to enlarge my vision.

The completion of this project could not have been accomplished without the help of my faithful consultant and proofreader, Cathey Graham Nickell. She is the most encouraging and delightful person to work with. Thank you for being that Angel who was sent to rescue me when I had paused because of a blind spot. I could not have finished this project without you.

To my beloved Daddy, Mr. Deodath K. Maharaj, thank you for having instilled in me such treasured life lessons. He used to say, "Keep your hands open when praising God so that you can be more of a blessing to others from the gifts which He gives to you. Whatever you are blessed with, never feel as if it is something you cannot part with to make another person smile."

Finally, a special thank you to both of my parents for sharing with me the necessary wisdom to keep strong and not complain about my trials, but rather, to rise above them. I am blessed to have my family, friends and colleagues. Thank you for your continuous prayer and loving thoughts. I receive your well wishes and believe that happiness will become a reality for me in this life.

How Writing Can Heal:

FROM THE EXPERTS

I believe poems that are written with the intention to heal can provide renewed strength—psychologically, emotionally and physically to those who are receptive. The depth of intuitive wisdom contained in each line can help to transform one's subconscious thoughts of defeat into more tangible manifestations of healing at a conscious level.

"Poetry brings unconscious forces into consciousness to make them understandable...It provides an outlet for emotions." – *Owen Heninger*

"Writing with deep feeling improves immune system function, decreases stress, lowers blood pressure, and increases positive short- and long-term mood changes." – *James W. Pennebaker, Ph.D., Writing to Heal: A Guided Journal for Recovering from Trauma and Emotional Upheaval*

"You willed yourself to where you are today, so will yourself out of it." – *Stephen Richards*

"Not only can you learn to listen to your body, you can—with practice—tell your body how you want it to feel. You can regain control, something everyone with pain wants: to control your life again and put pain in the back seat." – *The American Pain Association Chronicle*

"Remember, the purpose of the pain is to divert attention from what's going on emotionally and to keep you focused on the body." – *John E. Sarno, M.D., The Mindbody Prescription: Healing the Body, Healing the Pain*

"Be yourself. Above all, let who you are, what you are, what you believe, shine through every sentence you write, every piece you finish." – *John Jakes*

"Writing is a form of personal freedom. It frees us from the mass identity we see in the making all around us. In the end, writers will write not to be outlaw heroes of some underculture but mainly to save themselves, to survive as individuals." – *Don Delillo*

Author's Note

My heart's intention for writing this book started out as a way to help my own children. Children of divorced parents are often unsure about how to cope with the negative emotions they experience from the deep-rooted pain that comes when a certain comfort zone is threatened. The life change of divorce stirs up inner turmoil, which can lead to unresolved internal battles. This often creates confusion that takes on physical manifestations in our daily performance. I tried to seek professional counseling for my sons, but I could not afford it. The children also were uncomfortable speaking with others about what was going on within them. I contacted a renowned church for counseling, but they could not offer help unless both parents accompanied the children. I needed to find a way to reassure my sons that they should not blame themselves for what happened between their father and myself. I prayed for them to feel comfortable enough to express themselves to me without feeling judged.

I felt as if I was at the end of my rope in my attempts to find external help for my sons. So, I decided to try something that has helped me to cope with many negative experiences throughout my life. A coping tool that has not failed me to this day. It seemed farfetched; I thought that this was more of a girl's way of dealing with things, but it was my only option at the time. Having two boys who are often told by other males that being sensitive is not an acceptable emotion to express, left me a bit hesitant. I went out on a limb and asked the boys if they would be open to my helping them express themselves in a different way. A way that would also help them to share their deep inner selves with the only One who can ultimately help them—God! The boys responded that it was okay so long as no one discovered what was going on in their lives at a personal level. After sharing some examples of how this works and how it can become an instrument—an instrument that consciously transformed my own life one day at a time—my sons were willing to give it a try.

This coping mechanism helps me deal with so many of life's uncontrollable and unpredicted ups and downs. It allows me a medium through which I can talk things out; it helps me to harbor very few negative emotions. I knew from an early age that it was only through God whom I could speak to about my deep-rooted pain, my broken heart and my secrets without fear of judgment. I learned that God is my best friend. I did not need to look far when I needed Him, nor did I have to make a phone call or ask if He had the time to chat. He has never failed in bringing me comfort at the end of each conversation. After discovering that God resides inside me and that I am never alone, I became empowered by His grace. My faith and love led me to discover the most reliable counselor for myself and now for my precious boys.

I often spend quiet time with God, hashing out all that disturbs me. Thought-provoking challenges creep up so often that I sometimes think I am losing life's battle without resolve. It is in these moments of self-torture, when I feel as if I cannot not handle a second more, a silent whisper on the inside encourages me to surrender it all to Him. He made me happy, healthy and whole most often when I was sad. I felt like a child who had lost her way home and could not remember her address. On those nights when I felt left out in the cold with no true friends to turn to, God placed a blanket of love over me and kept my heart warm with kindness, compassion and love for others until I was able to feel for myself again. God surrounded me with words that flashed before me like beacons of light through books and audios from genuine God-seeking souls; people like Pastor Joel Osteen, Dr. Wayne Dyer, Dr. Deepak Chopra, Oprah Winfrey, Marianne Williamson, Pastor Nick Vujicic and other how-to-live guidelines shared by the Self Realization Fellowship. I was able to gather solid stones of wisdom that, to this day, continue to pave my way to a home far greater than the address I seemed to have forgotten.

God's perfect counsel is free, and He promises that He will lessen my load when it becomes too heavy. He loves me unconditionally, regardless of what I've done or how I've fallen short in my undertakings. It is this inner reassurance that has brought me peace, and I'm now able to regain great strength in God through the spoken words of those above-mentioned individuals in my moments of weakness. Their perfectly timed, God-sent words resonate deep within, reminding my soul of its true nature and its ability to become enlightened in this life.

Each day, I made a conscious decision to say to myself on awaking, "Today I am placing all my trust and faith in God; I am happy, I am healthy, I am whole, and I am healed. I surrender my all to Him who gives me this strength!" The more I vigilantly practiced surrendering my daily everything to

God before the day began, the more my trust and faith grew. I learned to actively carry God's presence consciously with me wherever I went. I did my best to sustain my thoughts of pleasing Him with all of my words and actions throughout in every way. This was not an easy task, but I can be stubborn at times; when I speak faith-filled words over my life, I do whatever I need to do, so that I leave no excuses for myself.

As often as I fell throughout the day, I forgave myself and told myself to try again—not later, but—in that very moment. I did not allow myself to stay in the darkness of my own ignorance for long because I knew that only God was able to do for me what no man can, even if he tried. He breathes a breath of life again into this once-shriveling heart. He gives me reason to want to live, not for myself, but in order to be a living example of God's grace and faithfulness to us. He will deliver to you more than you can imagine for your life if you give your relationship with Him a chance to be your first priority. God gave me the strength to do my best, to begin to take some control of my life again as He ultimately is the one in control of it all, and I was able to stand back and look at His plans unfold right before me. He now reveals His purpose for my life in each moment—a fate that this world could not have offered me independently of itself.

My way of communicating with God began at a personal level. I wrote many "Dear God" letters from the young age of eleven, imagining Him to be a friend in a faraway land. I used the letters as one would drop notes to some organization in a complaint, praise or suggestion box. Those letters were discarded within a few days or weeks of writing them, because I feared that one of my family members would find them and ridicule me. I later learned about metaphors and analogies in school. My heart filled with excitement, realizing that I could write to God in such a way that, if anyone read the writings, they would not know exactly what was taking place in my life. In this way, I could feel safe. I began to write in the form of poetry; I wasn't sure if poetry was what I was writing, but it seemed to take on a poetic tone when I read them to God. This began a conscious transformation within me without premeditation.

I now use poetry to teach my own children to express themselves and to release their inner emotions to God. A few of the poems in this book were written on behalf of my children, in Part Two, to help them develop their own personal relationship with God. I wanted my sons to know that God is someone who is approachable and that He can be their best friend. He can do above and beyond what any one person can ever do for them, including myself. He is the only One who clearly sees the condition of their hearts, knows their darkest secrets and still loves them unconditionally.

No matter how we view the experiences in our lives—both positive and negative—they are sent for us to gain wisdom and direction on how to return to the place that God has chosen for our home. God has given each of us a free will to choose, and it is up to us to know whom we should turn to in times of need and in times of praise for the things that bring us joy and success. This interactive healing journal was initially written to help a few people with their pain similar to that of myself and of my children. It has now been transformed into a tool that can speak to the soul of readers at a deeper level, from all walks of life. It was not written for any one particular religion, race or social status. It will help you to see how intimate your relationship with God or Spirit can become. It will allow you to silence yourself in order to intuitively hear the unspoken wisdoms in response to your soul call, which is translated and understood with the language of your heart.

This poetic approach to healing helps to consciously transform who we are and how we view ourselves so that we can become who God desires for us to be. I pray that these poems will help shed those negative emotions in your life that can possibly become toxic to the mind, body and spirit. I pray that you develop a trust in God knowing that He will take care of you; know without a shadow of doubt, that He sees every tear you have shed and will rescue you from depression, self-pity, anger and un-forgiveness. He will fill your life with light and love. Believe with a radical and intense faith that He will help you pave a new way when the old one seems to have gotten you lost. God will exchange your heavy burdens with His endless wisdom and love.

It is through this God-given conscious transformation, which is taking place within me, that I seek to bring forth the light and love of God to you. So that you may shine brilliantly with the illumination of the ever-so-pure soul qualities already existent within you!

— Marla Maharaj

Dear Readers,

I pray that this book can assist you on your path of pilgrimage within. May it expand the hearts of those in need and be an instrument of love and healing. Allow these moments of deep and profound silence to change the way you think and transform who you are into whom God has created you to be. Have faith in God; meditate on His wisdom and teachings. Surrender your all to Him. Sincerely pray, "Lord, let Thy will be done in my life according to your loving desires."

— Marla

"Make the Lord the shepherd of your soul. Make Him your searchlight when you move along a shadowy pathway in life. He is your moon in the night of ignorance. He is your sun during the wakeful hours. And He is your polestar on the dark seas of mortal existence. Seek His guidance.

The world will go on like this in its ups and downs. Where shall we look for a sense of direction? Not to the prejudices aroused within us by our habits and the environmental influences of our families, our country, or the world; but to the guiding voice of truth within."

Paramahansa Yogananda
The Divine Romance

Table Of Contents

Part One

Part Two

Part Three

Quotes from those who inspire you:

Part One

Consciously Building a Relationship With God

Start by doing what's necessary;
then do what's possible;
and suddenly you are doing
the impossible.

It is no use walking anywhere
to preach unless our walking is
our preaching.

- Francis of Assisi

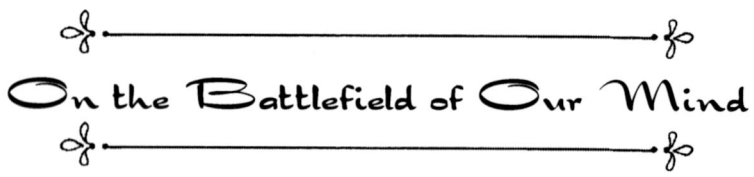

On the Battlefield of Our Mind

Never-ending battles in the mind
Hearts wounded, lives entwined
A warfare fought in ignorance
Authorities overthrown by our benevolence

Bodies weakened from senses blind
Soldiers stand strategically aligned
Overlooking the wisdom of what takes precedence
Ego builds our false confidence

Straightening our frame and silencing our mind
Leaving past memories consciously behind
With efforts sincerely made to regain our intelligence
We stake claims to distinguish our providence

Narrowing our focus on peace re-defined
Spirit resurrected and energies combined
Techniques modified to increase our tolerance
Reminding ourselves of our spiritual significance

On the battlefield of our mind
Succumb not to darkness enshrined
Traveling progressively, establishing a balance
Golden stars of wisdom exchanged for our perseverance

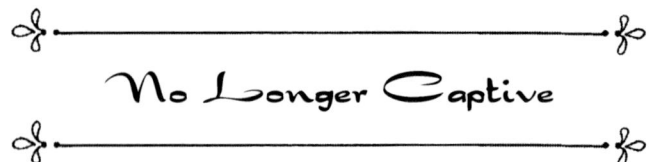

No Longer Captive

Many has been the days of bondage and fear
Those days where your love did not seem near
I would show up ready at your front door
Only to run away after hearing other footsteps on the floor
Scared and in panic, I would hide in the dark
Praying that these terrifying mental voices would leave without a mark
Can you turn on the lights for me, Father?
I am still here; it is "I" your daughter
I see you in me and I know that I am free
It's just that these narrow hallways frighten me
If you could leave the lights on in our house
I will return this time without being as timid as a mouse
I am learning of your spiritual law
What it means to love and to be loved without a flaw
Love has always been your number one tool
Teach me to use it as an extension of your grace, and not be a fool
Protect me with your armor Lord and keep me from all harm
I trust that my destiny has already been written in your palm
I am a little older now and have grown to know you more
I will no longer allow those dreadful voices to restrain me from
patiently waiting at your door
The distance of my heart's desire which once seemed like years
Have now been shortened by my increasing faith and cleansing tears
I am no longer captive; my victory is here
I am anointed and appointed; your love causes me to no longer live in fear
Lord, accept my love, for in this life I surrender
And may the words, "thy will be done within me," be all I silently utter

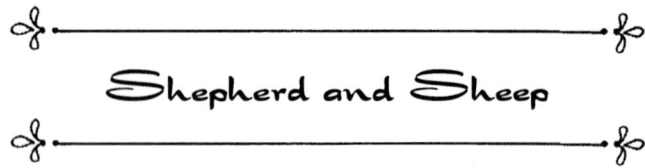

Shepherd and Sheep

Guide me Father and help me to see
That I am in you and you are in me
As your sheep, I often go astray and run off track
Lead me with your rod of discipline so that I may safely make it back

I and the Father are one of a kind
I won't allow delusions to overtake the character of my mind
Your miracles are necessary to redeem the once spiritually blind
I am blessed to know you with my love aligned

You are my light and my wisdom
You are my only truth to attaining eternal freedom
My physical body may be entangled in things of this world
But do keep my Christ consciousness in you unfurled

Dear shepherd, draw me by your love and keep it real
Allow my awareness of you at times, so tangible I can feel
Carry this my serving spirit to its mission complete
For this sheep you've cared for; it's only the love of my Shepherd I seek

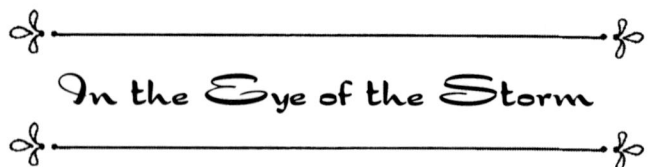

In the Eye of the Storm

Raging waves, roaring wind
Fearfully I take shelter within
Hiding safely from life's storms
Evacuating routes, re-establishing man's norm

Adrenaline secreted as a response naturally
As threat of danger lurks in thoughts outside of Thee
Ego-created delusions fill my mind
With etchings of a false reality determined to keep my senses blind

Before all faith is lost in my habitual past
The dark skies no longer look overcast
The gentleness of a breeze sweeps on by
Positioning me perfectly under God's watchful eye

Anxiously awaiting what happens next
Will my attitude and perseverance stand the test?
Will I remember to pause then and take in God's true reality?
Or will I waste time on my very own futility?

Cherishing these precious moments that are left
Life's storm may have passed, but it's not over yet
Securing all that is valuable and of highest priority
Reminds one that it's only God's love that is of guarantee

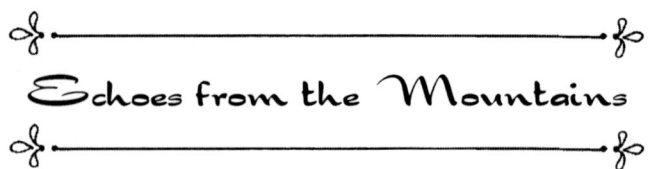

Echoes from the Mountains

When life seems down, as it sometimes will,
When the harder you work, the more things seems to roll downhill
When the light you once knew, now seems distant from you
You will soon realize that it's a mountain you're on; look ahead of you.

Give thanks to God for bringing you this far on your path
His intention is meant to bless you; it's not His wrath
Never once have you not been provided for
Nor has He ceased any opportunity, before closing an expired door.

Open your eyes and see His grace
It is the closest you will get to seeing God's beautiful face
Take pleasure in seeking Him who knows you by name
For His unfailing love is one and the same.

Listen for His soft echoes as He calls out you
His promises are faithful and His words deliver that which is true
Be still and know that He will always be there
Assert yourself with confidence knowing that God can take you anywhere.

There is hope to find in so many different places
Don't get discouraged because you have not found it on many human faces
Never give up, for this is all a part of your test
Mentally reliving our shortcomings, until we have chosen His best.

Each day find at least one thing to be grateful for
With each recall, He gives great visions of a new life to explore.

My...

My Beloved
May the scars of my trials, which I deserve
Cause me to come to you saying, "How may I serve?"

My Father
Bruised and in fear I allowed myself to be pushed around in the darkness
In search of your light, I beg your forgiveness

My Friend
When the world lifted me up and threw me aside
I found safety in the comforts of your arms, on your shoulders I cried

My Lover
As wildflowers grew uncontrollably in my garden, I was bewildered,
"What am I to do?"
Suddenly, I looked upon my life and smiled;
in loving devotion I would offer those very petals to you

My Redeemer
My very help in times of need, you gave me the soil and instructed me
on how to plant your seed
You blessed my harvest and even helped to pluck the weeds;
all along you were my lead

My Savior
You came just in time to rescue me from this desolate land
I am forever grateful for your loving grace and know now that my life
is completely in your hand

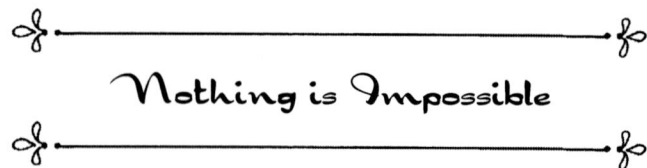

Nothing is Impossible

Falsely we believe our ego as true
Leading us time after time into a darkened hue
Blinded by our ignorance we are led astray
Held captive by our pride; a life we so boldly portray

Awestruck by sharp corners and dead ends unforeseen
We double back in fear wanting to alter the motion picture on the screen
As the movie rolls we realize that this was all meant to be
Life's experiences individually patented especially for you and me

Misled by delusions we proclaim an end
Forgetting our soul's natural compulsion to transcend
Remember Home, Remember Me
An inner voice of silence whispers, "Nothing is impossible with Thee!"

Abandon your mind and all of its thoughts
It is your enemy for the pain and suffering it's brought
Love is the only trait that will undeniably sustain
Impossible is not our true nature; it's our own mental restrain

Master Key

Lord help me to not be careless once more
Teach me to wait steadfastly at your door
Allow me to acknowledge you in all that I do
For whatever I do unto others, I also do unto you

When I needed support, you held my hand
And carried me through this desolate land
You took me in and with love you consoled
Your divine spirit trapped in this human mold

Weakened from hunger you gave me food
Naked I came unto you and you understood
Trapped like a prisoner in my own inescapable cell
You gave me your Master Key and reassured me that all will be well

Save me from these seemingly endless cycles of reincarnations
Punishments and rewards are a result of my own actions
Help me to see that with each error I consciously make
I'm delaying my journey back home and it's a risk that I take

The Room Inside

Bright are the things in front of me
Unsure of the details of those distant and difficult to see
Battling between thoughts of this present century
I choose for now to focus less on my memory

Shelves filled with gifts of life's varieties
Some compartments remain abandoned from adversities
Structures erected to support that which really mattered
Too much emphasis was placed on things that got scattered

As a spectator looking in
I can now give this room a new spin
Discarding the broken and dusting what's left
This temple will no longer be classified as bereft

Tears of joy and of pain
Collection of prayers and senses restrain
Both given with intentions of love and grace
It's man's divine purpose to live in the light of this God-given place

Through the window of introspection
I ask God to guide my intuition
Let me see the future as not filled with fear
Help me to keep my thoughts of His presence ever so near

Misunderstood

Miracles are given especially to those who cannot see
The unconditional love given to you and me
It is a love that is equally shared
But not often received as spiritually paired

What is the significance of a miraculous sign?
While mendaciously exhibiting faith, impeding your divine incline
Allowing for a few metaphysical apparitions of sounds, visions, and light
To smother our center of consciousness from its own freedom plight

Stop this instance and take heed to that which is real
It is only God's grace and love revealed
Forsake your ego and your wealthy pride
As the intentions of your heart will remain untried

Overconsumption of material and sense pleasures
We delay our rightful claim to God's unlimited treasures
It is not just given to the humble and the good
It is the integration of his way of life into ours that's often misunderstood

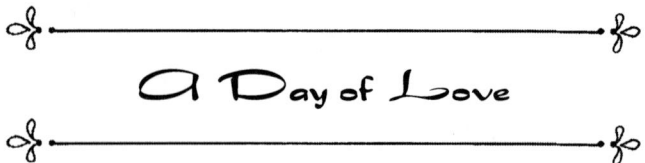

A Day of Love

A day of love…is that all we have to spare?
Why not carry this torch each day of the year?

Maybe we are too busy or have some unexplained excuse
Either way a love not given, is a love misuse

God's love is real and it is for all to see
So why hold onto it? Just set it free

When love is given and pain is received
It is a love falsely taken with expectations preconceived

I cannot imagine the tears, which God's heart has shed
For our unkind words and un-forgiveness to others we have not spared

A day of love may not make it all right
But it can let someone special know that you will not give up without a fight

Let love and light be your guide
And let this day of love be renewed with the One in which you secretly confide

Butterflies

Dear God, how did I come to be?

Much bigger than I thought of me

At first I knew I had no wings

Now my wings are more important than most things

Dear God, how did I come to see?

This light that is inside of me

For quite some time I was engulfed by darkness with no way out

Now I am free to learn a bit more about what life's about

Dear God, how did I come to know?

That your love for me is an overflow

Growing up, I thought that more love was given to only the best

But it's only now that I see, that too was a test

Dear God, how did I come to be so confident?

Enabling myself to be used as your instrument

With color and grace and beauty encased

One smile, one giggle, one spirit graced

Dear God, how did I find true love so naturally?

As if it has always been a part of me

Loving you has kept me thirsty

Living for You has taught me to say, "You are so worthy!"

Constant Communion

A Hunger arises inside to remain in your presence
In spite of life's trial, I do not lose confidence
I am cradled in the warmth of your compassion
Robed in your armor, your love displayed in my action

Painted on the canvas of my soul
Colors often graciously applied, never seem to grow old
Hues so vivid, once hidden by these worldly seeking eyes
Now transparently revealing life's beautiful disguise

My soul established with an inheritance of dominion
Achieving all of which I desire through our divine communion
Years of darkness vanishes from my sight
Unbearable burdens now seem to disappear on this eagle's flight

Disciplined by the dagger of your wisdom
You shear the veils of my delusion, exposing the world through your vision
Humbled by the experience of our constant communion
You remain ever wrapped in my thoughts, as my divine companion

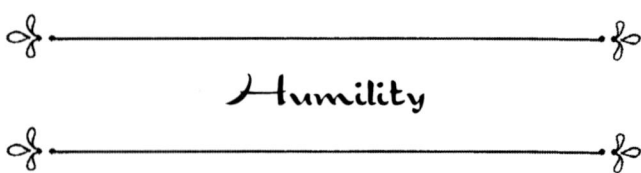

Humility

Forgiveness and compassion are Godly attributes
Qualities that our spiritual lives contribute
Not only to those who give you praise and fame
But to those, whom to you, they criticize and blame

Even when words spoken are untrue and unjustified
Cease our words and actions before being mortified
Whether praise or blame, let God be the judge
Giving to your ego, a prudent nudge

When anger is present and misunderstanding grows
Under the influence of emotions, wisdom goes
Allow a few minutes for antagonism to calm
Encouraging open-mindedness instead of a state of alarm

Seeking understanding at the hand of motives impure
You justify your own convictions at ego's allure
Consider listening to the heart of a friend in need
Exemplify God's wisdom instead, by planting a new seed

Inner Change

Inwardly we need to focus on our own advancement
As unsolicited counsel can create much resentment
Imposing our will on others of intentional defiance
Inhibits Spiritual counsel, unless one is seeking guidance

When the trials of life become overpowering
Being humble and wise is encouraged through inner surrendering
Being a reflection of what you want others to be
Can speak volumes to other souls seeking to be free

God gave to each of us our own intellection
Blessed in silence to create in Him our very own companion
Excuse our expectation of the world to change recognizably
Let us change ourselves first and our environment will shift remarkably

Inner changes are magnified in our unique outer self
Eminent and unequivocally recognized when finding oneself
With much humility and divine wisdom we surrender to who we have become
Fine examples of soul qualities; victorious warriors of whatever may come

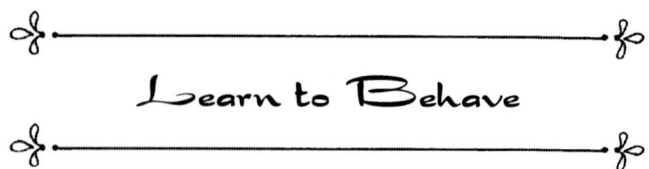

Learn to Behave

Seems so difficult to learn to behave
And not to keep the soul as a body bound slave
It is not the soul who displays these actions
It is the habit of our undisciplined minds and thoughtless reactions

Learn to cultivate soul qualities within
Do not allow life's stumbles to make doubtful our win
We are not merely mortal beings; we are divine
And our soul wants to remind us of our unique design

Allow not this life to go to waste
Our soul remains thirsty, for the consciousness of God's love it has taste
It is nourished by God's divine nectar
Let our behavior complement our soul's elixir

Be an example of God in the lives of others
Relationships are destroyed when love smothers
See the soul flowers within ourselves before we teach
Then improve the quality of our own lives with a loving outreach

Doing My Best

I will do my best in every moment of every day
I will not be discouraged and give up in dismay

When the trials of life are felt in each moment
It is the shadow of God's outstretched hands ever present

Instead of running from the dualities of this world
I will experience them in my consciousness and cherish them as I would gold

Obstacles are placed as opportunities on my path
They are not meant to be full stops; but a new start

Wisdom will come when I patiently await
The delusion to be removed from my mind's unstable state

God grant me the serenity so that I may be free
As I repeatedly surrender my daily stresses to Thee

Forgive me, Lord, let me hold on to no wrong
Let my heart listen for the beautiful calling of my soul's song

For in its unspoken lyrics, I am guided to seek you within
In this sacred temple of unconditional love, I can clearly feel your presence therein

Mirrors

Smudges on the mirror of my mind
Cause me to see myself as ugly and unkind
Old habits of being concerned of how others see me
Keeps my consciousness shackled and not free

With a spritz of God's unconditional Love and positive affirmation
I can spend time in introspection enhancing this illusory reflection
Balancing this mind and its emotions, I can respond to God's call
I can see His spirit's confidence within me, now standing tall

Crystal clear without a blemish
I can choose to see myself as God's masterpiece, finished
Using discrimination to improve my abilities
Daily starving my weaknesses; with discipline, I prioritize my responsibilities

Failures and flaws plant a desire for increasing self-improvement
With a deep inner conviction I can change this inner environment
Recognizing many of these undesirable traits
I continue to polish this mirror as God's beauty in me awaits

These smudges that are seen on the mirrors of my mind
I will clean and polish daily with His words, so kind
Determined to see His love and light shine brilliantly through
Lord, help me to clean this mirror to better reflect you

Expectations

God's expectations of us are as simple as can be
Spending time with Him but not to a lesser degree
Put Him first in all that we do
And have faith that above all He is true

When placed in a trying situation and ready to react
Developing self-control helps to mentally retract
We can choose to stir this tasteless brew
Or we can answer God's call when He asks, "Who are you?"

Giving another control over our emotions
May not be best when aspiring for spiritual promotions
God's discipline is strictly one of a kind
No matter how it is presented, we must learn to keep an even mind

Our duty is to correct ourselves so that we may grow
Being critical, angry and judgmental of others, are not good qualities to sow
Wisdom taught by our God given experiences is priceless
When we anchor ourselves in Him who is changeless

Thoughts

Inwardly thinking of God through our thoughts
Can help to loosen those stubborn mental knots
That stifle our consciousness with worldly things
And promise to deliver a life of happiness, which it never brings

Guiding our thoughts by drawing them from a higher power
Is a far better guarantee of satisfaction when our spirit is sour
Keeping our minds focused and centered
We surrender our lives; within your temple we've entered

Not swaying when facing tremendous obstacles
We gain strength in taking the limits off our spiritual muscles
We find within ourselves much faith and courage
When we choose not to resist the experiences God desires for our voyage

The efforts we make in keeping our minds affixed
Shows our all-pervading God, that our love is transfixed
In the presence of our silent hearts we vow
Not to be satisfied with anything less than God; to Him alone we bow

Never Give Up

Immerse your thoughts in God alone
Let not your responsibilities be neglected without this tone
No need to run and hide from the trials of this world
It is in those experiences you'll find God's wisdom more precious than Gold

Faith in God is one of your needs
With daily prayer and meditation we can plant our spiritual seeds
Living a life surrendering to God's will
Will lessen our troubles and keep our spirit at peace and still

Take rest in knowing that God's work has already begun
No need to come repeatedly to Him singing the same sad song
We can live and take action and keep our being with God
Allow Him to guide us lovingly with his disciplinary rod

Never give up on finding God inside
It is in our self-created distractions He hides
Pull aside the curtains that keep the darkness at play
Allow God's light to shine within us, His brilliant display

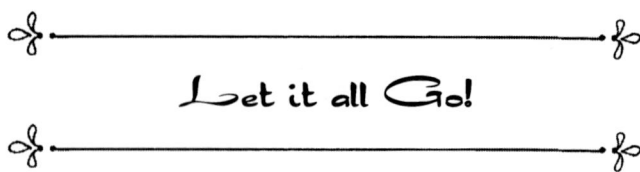

Let it all Go!

Inviting memories of past mistakes to poison our lives
Gives the enemy a footstool by which he thrives

Never be discouraged or downcast by others' judgment of us
Nor allow our past mistakes to reflect an image of disgust

Know that when we've accepted forgiveness, God has wiped clean our slate
Renewed our spirit, so that we may now serve Him from a new plate

The things of our past do not matter at all
What we become through them is really our own call

All experiences are presented so that we may learn
Change ourselves within them and wisely we will discern

Persist not further in the errors of our ego
Surrender to His guidance when He says, "Let it all go!"

Succumb not to our own understanding, for it is flawed
Rise instead to a divine living, one that will bring us success in our search for God

God's Care

God brings to us, all of our experiences
Our good, our ills and even our sacrifices
Seeing all people as equally his instruments
Opens our minds to the range of his omnipresence

The hands of God can be seen behind all that happens
He is the one who lifts our spirits and also the one that dampens
He silently watches over every move we make
Every experience is a blessing and there are no mistakes

In the stillness of the night as we daily introspect
Our successes and failures to Him we give; have no regrets
God is nearer than our nearest as we begin to see
Each breath taken is a blessing offered to us by Thee

Do not allow our worldly duties to constantly crowd our mind
We have a higher priority, one of a divine kind
Meditate and give all of our responsibilities back into God's care
Give all things to God with a heart sincere

Divine Destiny

Feelings of being unfulfilled
Maltreating our souls as if immature and unskilled
Blinded we ignore the divine image within
Allowing matter consciousness to penetrate our skin

Our divine destiny is to know God, alas
With light and love there is no need for an atlas
Nourishing this yearning with loyalty and dedication
We manifest in our daily lives our spiritual affirmation

Striving for constant humility
Seeking as our first priority
Pretending to follow his path is living carelessly
Our benefits are endless as we live for Him consciously

When problems arise, concentrate on that single point
All answers will come with wisdom He's anointed
Scatter your mind not on self-attuned fears
Take all to God for your divine destiny He bears

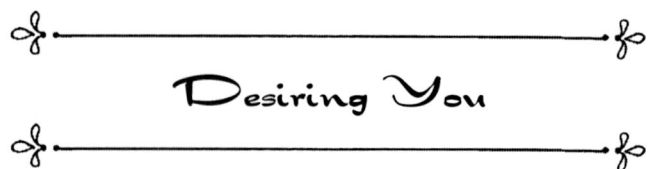

Desiring You

Heavenly Father I want so much to know you more
But do my actions reveal that desire in its core?
Favoring you with just mere words and an occasional thought
May not be the best way your attention is sought

Silently I must churn the ether
With loving devotion I will not falter
Disciplining my senses more and more each day
Lord, help me to not let this world lead me astray

Desiring to spend more time with you I will cultivate
Half-hearted efforts are not appropriate
Bless me with a vision that I can hold onto in my mind
Even the sight of your outline shadow of some kind

Give me the strength to hold onto your thoughts one hundred percent
As my soul progresses along its spiritual assent
Surround me with constant reminders of you
Let me prove to this disobedient ego that you are so true

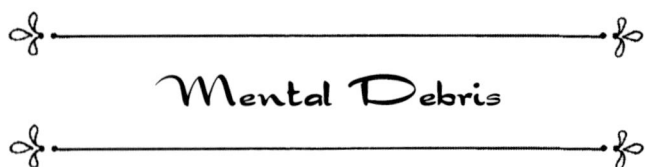

Mental Debris

Mindless thoughts of likes and dislikes
We stunt our growth and delay our spiritual spikes
Wasting our time deciphering mental webs we have spun
When time runs out what good have they done?

God assigns us infinite opportunities
To come to Him first, bringing our weighted necessities
He is shy and will not stand in our way
His deliverance to all is promised but why do we not stay?

What a great delusion we live in
With innumerable chances we still hesitate to begin
Like tumbling weeds our thoughts are tossed
We gamble our lives at what incremental cost?

Foolishly we allow our minds to drift on the sea
Carrying with it mounds of mental debris
We are not will-o'-the-wisps travelling in the dark
Why not ignite this mental debris with His inner spark?

My Soul Call

Oh how my soul calls out to me
Disguised in thoughts of fulfilling some material fantasy
It is the soul's nature to communicate through love and to live up to its name
This is not entirely my selfish desire that I proclaim

Aspiring to achieve these ambitious goals
Only reveals the soul qualities of my Master's molds
Secretly sending messages to and from our self-created world
By faith I listen to stories of a lifetime of journeys being unfold

My soul knows to seek ye first the kingdom of God
The world does not deliver what it advertises, yet it is the one most applaud
Taking on this challenge to find the truth, regardless of what others may see
Is a guidance promised by the source of our soul; not a fleeting fantasy

Not afraid of asking God for all my soul's needs
His wisdom's planted; it is His desire I nurture in the form of these seeds
With His unfailing love my soul no longer craves for much of anything
For His all-inclusive satisfaction of a life fulfilled is most captivating

I find myself travelling this world in search of all I seek
Only to discover in its temporary pleasures, that my soul is still incomplete
There is no amount of human love that can bribe my soul to being satisfied
What a great loss it will be for my soul, if its soul call I have denied

Divine Mother

Divine Mother, so caring and so kind
Impress your purity upon my mind
Be thou merciful and full of Grace
It's your power of divine love I wish to embrace

Like an insistent child I come to you
My faith-filled request will be granted as I pursue
Never giving up, I do my part
Thou art the flame of your love on the altar of my heart

You deposit your seeds of intelligent awareness
Your motherly instinct guides me with a feeling of tenderness
Vibrating your divinity in all of creation
I am enthralled by your limitless expansion

Both Father and Mother, you are the Cosmic One
Planted in the womb of the Father, Holy Spirit and Son
A universal matrix of your manifestation
In silence I witness the ultimate truth of your procreation

Part Two

Transformation by Example

Strength does not come
from winning.

Your struggles develop
your strength.

When you go through hardships
and decide not to surrender,
that is strength.

- Mahatma Gandhi

I Don't Care...!
I Love You the Most...

I say I don't care because I am hurting

And my age limits my words from reasserting

I am told that I am too small

So my opinions seem to not matter at all

How can my voice be heard

When all that I mention, is viewed as absurd?

You may not think so, but I did grow

And my eyes see the world as its bestow

I know that the world is not a child's play

I listen to God's words and I choose to not go astray

I may be your child, but I am God's too

The truth is; God's light dwells in both me and you

I know that once we are born, we too will die

So why not live each day as if it's our final goodbye?

Why speak to me as if I have no sense?

Only to cover your own flaws, you put up this defense

I need you to understand that I am not only yours

God's spirit inside of me; seeps through my very pores

So why treat me the way you often do

When that image of God inside of you, is reflected in me too?

I am of no lesser worth than you make it seem

I too am trying to make the best out of God's dream

I have asked often for you to join my quest

Please take this time to listen to my heart's request

Come travel with me on this voyage through life

No matter what happens, together we can handle this strife

I can help dust you off when you fall

And you can teach me how to stand tall

I can let you know even when you're doing wrong

And you can show me the right way to stand strong

You may be older and wiser than I am

But we have our own test in life to pass God's exam

I may not be all that you would like to see

But one day I will have to travel across my own sea

God's love is all we need to make us whole

Come take this step towards Him with me; let's make this our goal

I am tired of carrying this weight on my own

I am only a child with a heart not made of stone

Help me to discover the truth of who I am

Let the shepherd guide you to raising his little lamb.

I pray that you can show me the way while I am still small

Because I love you the most, and that should mean something
for you to make this call

Can You See Me?
I Am Still Here

I look at how you treat others in your presence
How you respond to the relationship between us as one that of absence
Can't you find a different way to express that what I do is not your best?
And not openly expose the thing that rubs you the wrong way about me,
which you contest
I find it hard to truly be me when I am with you
I can hardly remember the times when you took interest in the things I like to do
I try to put on this show, so that I can be approved
Instead you have made up your mind to misunderstand me
and now you stand confused
It hurts so much to feel that I am not cared for in the same way
To not have the same love others feel from you brings me dismay
If expressing myself in this way sounds too sensitive to be one of your children
Then know that God has given me the strength of being one in a million
This pain I have seems to not leave me alone
I can feel a wall of defense being erected inside of me
on a foundation not fit for a throne
I don't want to be this way, I want to be kind
I want this lack of love, attention and appreciation to forever leave my mind
Unfairly treated and a bit rejected is how I feel
I am trying to find new ways to shake off this lack of zeal
I hear that God gives us abundantly all that we need
But when pressed down by this favoritism you show to others; not even God's
water seems to promote growth of this fruitful seed
Your approval and support means so much to me
It is the very thing that I need to unleash the God-given power needed to
nourish the root to this young tree

I have read many success stories between parents and their children
And I wonder if I will ever be able to say that my story is one of them
Just because I don't support some of your vices doesn't mean that I am wrong
Have you ever stopped to think that maybe my ideals are very strong?
It's not that I try to tell myself to not favor the things you seek
I do not hold the same prestige as those you consider your friends,
so I prefer to remain meek
It's hard to see my own beauty inside
When the harsh words thrown towards me never think to hide
I find myself hating me, because I feel as if I will never be good enough for you
I feel like I am losing the person I love; something that I wished never to be true
This pain inside is so hard for me to bear
I am a tree which God has planted in your life and I still need much care
This tone by which you speak to me weighs like a ton on my heart
And with a lack of loving words to balance, I can feel us being torn apart
As a kid, I should not be made to feel so much hate growing in me
Even the far-fetched thoughts of taking my own life, should never be
What can I do to help someone I love to understand
that life is a learning experience and we do not know it all?
But fall on my knees and cry, "Father! Help me to walk upright according to
your ways and not be afraid to stop this painful crawl!"
I may not be very old, but being twelve is enough
I thank you God for teaching me how to live through Him when life gets tough
I feel like I am dying inside, but I have chosen to live for you
Kindly prove to this heart of mine, Oh God,
that your promises are faithful and true
Can you see me? I am still here; the same child which God left in your care
Look at me and bear bold witness to your God-sent rightful heir
Help me father to not live in fear
Send me constant reminders, letting me know that you are here
Keep me safe and continue to use me as an instrument of your peace
This is my cry in life, Dear God, before this journey of mine ceases
I will declare that in this life, I will be victorious
Before this body dies, I will prove that God's desire for me was more glorious

Uniquely Me

Is my voice too weak that you cannot hear?
Or do you just choose to give me a deaf ear?
I am not you and I need for you to see,
That God has brought his own special assignment to me.

I try to keep a balanced mind in my head,
But each night my aching heart leaks tears on my bed.
How do I know that I have your support and direction?
When you wish not to stand with me while I listen to God's confirmation.

I ask God to help me and show me the way,
To not allow this world to lead me astray.
What you want for me may not be,
As long as you are not willing to join in agreement with God and me.

This life is not about us alone, as you know,
It is all just a few acts in God's grand show.
This scene may change from one clip to the next,
But we all remain His instruments, and with slight modifications,
He alters His text.

All About You

You claim that we come first in your life,
Yet your actions bring us much strife.
Why say these things when you don't mean it?
Why must this part of your play continue to air; just omit it!

We apologize if you think that we are wrong,
But it really hurts to be on the receiving end of this prong.
We often feel like a thorn on your side,
How much more of these painful emotions must we hide?

You have your temporary pleasures which you have succumbed to,
We are just kids and our voices seem to mean nothing to you.
We cry for help in so many ways that exposes what we see as true,
Why at this time when we need you the most,
it's less about us and more about you?

I've Lost My Voice

Stifled to say what is in my head
A feeling of heaviness fills my heart instead.

What can I do when I have lost my voice?
You never listen anymore, so what's my choice?

We seem to physically travel in the same direction,
But all of this we experience is such a delusion.

You distract me with bribes and other material things,
As happy as I may seem; what little temporary comfort it brings.

I would prefer instead that you would help me to find my voice,
To tell you how much I matter and that I too have a choice.

Not at will to express my upsetting emotions with all that you do,
Allow me some credit for having better self-control than you.

God, grant me the strength to stand when I am weak,
For I long to hear my loved-one say,
"Let's talk, my child, of the love that we both seek."

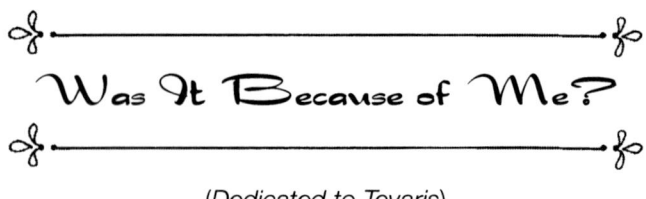

Was It Because of Me?

(Dedicated to Tevaris)

Lost in this world, not feeling mighty strong,
Tired of being blamed or needing to feel like I belong.
I try so very hard to fit in,
Maybe, I am just messed up from within.

Something is not right and I am not sure what it is,
Life at this age seems to be a never-ending quiz.
What have I done, Lord, to be placed in this position?
I was given no choice in this decision.

I have not seen my dad in such a long time,
I miss him and wonder if the melody of my sorrows will change its chime
I use to love to spend time with him watching television and all,
Those were priceless days when he gave me all of the reasons to stand tall.

I pray that God will help him to return his heart back home,
Because this sensitive heart of mine often feels pretty alone.
Carrying all the weight; we all just try to do our best
I know that this feels hard on us children, but this must also be our faith test.

Why Not Me?

I see the way you respond to me,
As though my worth is of lesser degree.
What have I ever done to you so wrong?
That you are not interested in listening to my heart's song.

Everyone else gets to see your brighter side,
But from me, a lot of it you hide.
Am I ugly and unkind?
That I give you many reasons to rid me off your mind.

I have tried to live up to your expectations,
But each time I fail, you boldly voice your condemnations.
How can I convince you that I have worth too?
When all you look to see is how much I do not reflect you.

I am trying this self-motivation thing I have heard about,
But all too often you leave me with so much doubt.
Why don't you encourage me in the same loving manner others see?
What is it that I am lacking; why not me?

I will continue to do what God has shown me is His best,
I somehow will gain enough courage to pass this part of life's test.
I will not let all of these painful tests carry me down,
God has promised me for overcoming all my trials, I will receive a crown.

Part Three

Listening for God's Spoken Wisdom Within

"Prayer is not asking.
Prayer is putting oneself in the
hands of God, at His disposition,
and listening to His voice in the
depth of our hearts."

- Mother Teresa

My Cup

My cup of sacrifice I give to you
For the remission of your sins I imbue
Cleansing you with the living blood of my divine energies
As I lift you from the pit of past seed tendencies

Those unable to partake of this communion
Attached to material intoxicants and sense stimulations
Temporarily feast at the table of spiritual degradation
Until dissatisfaction forces their hands to extend in oblation

Exchange your cross for a drink from my cup
Its delightful liberating taste you cannot dream up
Renounce your desires for senseless things
Let me trade your crucified ignorance for wisdom blessings

I will give you love for hatred and forgiveness for your wrongs
Come to me my precious child with your timely longing songs
Drink of my cup, let me quench your thirst
It is my promise fulfilled to keep you first

A Service of Love

I washed your feet with my very own hands
With love I did this; without any commands
A spirit of service I extend to you
A selfish and humble gesture; a love ever so true

Who is willing to exchange their life for my cross?
To have their hands pierced and embossed
These same hands, I served you with
I carried the weight of your sins and did not quit

My flesh was tempted by fear to tread this path
A voice responded, "This is your fate and not my wrath"
I am your son and must carry this flame
The light of my Christ Consciousness will be your highest acclaim

Humbly I serve all; even unto the least
I have cleansed you by my loving hands before the great feast
Grieve not my dear ones for I have served you well
And have sent my comforter that will forever in you dwell.

My Duty First

Make me first and you will see
What vast oceans flow from me
"Where there is a will, there is a way"
Hold on to my promises and you will not stray

The world is false and filled with delusion
Don't allow your emotion to enable spiritual confusion
When my spirit calls out you, you will know
There is nothing in this world that can prevent its flow

Be it family, be it friends, nothing else will precede
Nothing more appetizing than fulfilling my need
No duty greater than mine will you find
For the gifts and powers that you will be granted
will prove worthy to all mankind

Take your hands and place them in mine
Let me show you the blessings found in your unique inner designs
Let me help you along this journey within
You'll see what you're made of and who you've always been

Allow me to perform my duty first, before you leave me for this world
My love is warm and promising, not bitter and cold
I have given you a comparison to see light in the dark
So that you may freely choose to return to me your ever-loving spark

Only Love

I need one thing and one thing alone
A heart filled with love and not one of stone
I have no need for anything less
This is the one thing I seek, I must confess

I need your love and only love will do
Not a ritualistic superficial love, but one that is pure and true
There is nothing else in this world that will suffice
If it is not too much I ask of you, please make this small sacrifice

I would love to spend some waking moments with you
Where you can feel me consciously in the things that you do
Watching you share my love that flows through you unto others
Brings much Joy to my heart when that love is shared between parents,
friends and even lovers

I love you because you are my very own
I have created within you a heart so worthy for a throne
I gave you eyes so that I may see
Only the love of your soul returned to me

You can enter heaven with just this key of love
For heaven is within you and not just some place above
No amount of failures or fears will cause me to love you less
It is only when your love is given to me, that I am blessed

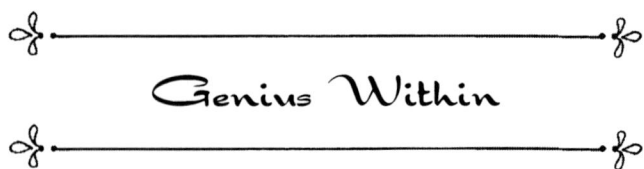

Genius Within

Look inside and you will see
You are simply a reflection of me
My Divinity flows harmoniously through you
Challenge yourself and you will find this to be true

Life's troubles allow for resilience
Setting the stage your spiritual convenience
Never a moment should you drop your chin
Position yourself to welcome your soul's twin

Awaken to who you truly are
A breathtaking vision of a morning star
Discarding all mental entrapments of the original sin
Prepare yourself to rediscover your genius within

My Dear Master, My Friend, My Guru

What does it mean to reflect you;
to have the slightest honor of slipping into your shoe?

Or maybe the question should be,
do I even deserve to gaze my eyes upon you?

Teach me your ways my Lord and help me to learn it well,
For some of these experiences I endure, surely feels like a taste of hell

Grant me peace and satisfaction in performing my duties
guided by your wisdoms
Shield me from the world's temptuous phantoms.

Being teased by frequent past inclinations and sense distractions,
I am aware of being pulled through false relationships,
into a hole of delusions.

Let your spirit of discernment take control of these wild reigns of my mind,
Please lovingly pull me back to you, for my unintentional thoughts of
deceiving you are nothing but rude and unkind.

I would prefer to be disciplined and learn to listen to your truth
Even though it's hard to accept at times,
you promise to deliver to me the only sooth.

I know that you would not forsake me nor lead me astray,
but this jet plane path to self-realization can often be a dismay.

Others are claiming to experience these self-expansions
with so little effort of their own,
Why do you choose to put me through these many steps
before I can open the doors to your home?

What kind of friend leads me unto a path with blindfolds covering my eyes?
Leaving me to feel lonely at times in darkness
with my own mind created demise.

Thinking not from my head, but with my heart,
Maybe it is the one friend who's lived his life
so that I would not be set apart.

Give me vision to recognize your grace and mercies in my life,
Restrain my steps, but strong be my will
to patiently bear the pains of your chiseling knife.

Surround me with spiritual company, firmly planted in their deeds,
Let their love, wisdom and companionship be the environment I choose
to nurture these fruitful seeds.

As difficult as this spiritual path may seem at times
I know that you will never leave me behind
because I am yours, and you are mine.

Thank you Master for our continuous divine friendship and forgiveness
I am your child trying to learn your ways; I am grateful for your kindness

My dear master, my friend, my guru, lead me by your light
Teach me to experience joy in communion with you
and taste the divine bliss of your sight.

Dear God,

Thank you God for listening to the cry of my soul call and healing me by your wisdom. Transform me within so that I may experience the power of your peace. Enter into my sacred temple where you already abide, and fill me with the joy of consciously being in the presence of your Holy Spirit. Help me to use my divine soul qualities to weave a fabric of unshakeable faith and hope in the lives of others. I remain anchored by your love. Receive these poems as flowers of my devotion as I lay them at Thy feet.

In Light and Love

Write Your Own Conscious Transformation Story Here:

Tear it out and mail to: Sharinglightandlove Press
                              P.O. Box 711254, Houston, TX 77271

AUTHORIZATION PAGE

Please check the one that applies to you

☐ I authorize the author to use my story in a future publication and it may include my name, city and state

Print Name _____

Authorization Signature _____

City, State_____

☐ I authorize the author to use my story in a future publication but would like my name to remain anonymous

Authorization Signature _____

☐ I do not authorize the author to use my story in a future publication. I only wish to share it with the author confidentially.

Would you like to get a response from the author?

Please include an address or P.O. Box.

CPSIA information can be obtained
at www.ICGtesting.com
Printed in the USA
FSOW02n2334140815
9806FS